North-East England

GRAEME PEACOCK

MYRIAD BOOKS

Lindisfarne Castle, Holy Island

The posts that stand in front of Lindisfarne Castle on Holy Island are the
remains of a jetty where lime was loaded onto ships bound for Dundee in
the 1870s. Further evidence of this trade can be found in the huge limekilns
still standing beneath the castle.

Built around the year 1550 from stones robbed from the nearby priory,
the castle was designed to offer protection to the harbour, which had
become a strategic naval base guarding against possible raids by the Scots.
It saw action during the Civil War and was briefly captured by two
supporters of the Scottish cause in 1715. Even though it continued to be
garrisoned it gradually declined and was last used by an artillery
detachment in the 1860s after which it began to fall into disrepair.

In 1902 the castle was bought by Edward Hudson, the founder of
Country Life magazine. He employed Sir Edwin Lutyens to restore the
building and convert it into a home. In 1944 the castle was given to the
National Trust.

Berwick-upon-Tweed

Trapped inside the Elizabethan walls of 1596 that enclose the town,
much of Berwick-upon-Tweed's ancient street pattern still survives. Parts
of Edward I's castle can still be seen, with its famous White Wall
descending down the hill towards the river like some medieval staircase. In
this violent period the town changed hands between England and Scotland
13 times before finally surrendering to the English in 1482.

The old harbour that played such an important part in the history
of Berwick is still to be seen with the wealthy merchants' houses and
doorways to their cellars cut through the walls. Just upstream, with its
arches reflected in the water, is the long narrow Old Bridge; its 15 arches
were built between 1611 and 1624. The bridge carried the Great North
Road until 1928 when the Royal Tweed Bridge with its four massive spans
of reinforced concrete was built to improve the flow of traffic.

Bamburgh Castle

Perched on its huge rock Bamburgh Castle can be seen for miles around; it dominates the pretty village below, clustered around its wooded green. The churchyard has a monument to Grace Darling together with the graves of victims of shipwrecks on the nearby Farne Islands.

The first known fortification here was a wooden palisade built around 547, although the site had been occupied since the Iron Age. The castle's name comes from that of Bebba, the wife of Ethelfrith who ruled Northumbria from 593 to 616, and it soon became known as Bebbanburgh. Its huge Norman keep has walls some 11ft (3m) thick; the building we see today is a combination of restoration by Lord Crewe, Bishop of Durham in the 18th century and then later by the first Lord Armstrong, the Victorian industrialist.

Standing on the shoreline and looking up to the castle it is easy to see why it is such a favourite with film directors. Its iconic status and the golden sands of the beaches below combine to make Bamburgh a magnet for visitors.

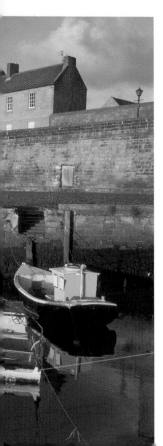

Seahouses

Pleasure craft and fishing vessels sit side by side in Seahouses harbour. Seahouses grew out of the village of North Sunderland when the fishermen built the "sea houses" by the side of the harbour.

The flat roof behind the old limekilns betrays the fact that a railway bringing the raw materials once terminated on top of it. The lime industry flourished up until the 1850s when the fishing industry took over, fuelled by the demand for herring – the demand was so great that in 1834 over 6,000 barrels of salted herring were dispatched to the Baltic States and Germany.

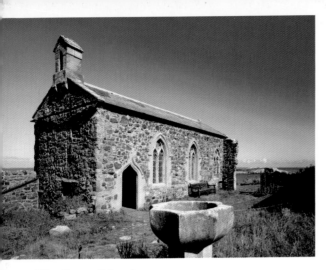

The Farne Islands

It was from the Longstone lighthouse that Grace Darling and her father rowed out to rescue the survivors of the shipwrecked *Forfarshire*. Flashing once every 20 seconds night and day the light was built between 1825 and 1826; it became fully automatic in 1980.

   The Farne Islands are owned by the National Trust and consist of a group of islands 2.5 miles (4km) off the fishing village of Seahouses; of these islands, between 15 and 28 are visible depending on the state of the tide, and they form one of Britain's most important seabird sanctuaries. The closest island is Inner Farne and the furthest out, at 4.4 miles (7km) from the shore, is Knivestone. The chapel on Inner Farne is built on the site of St Cuthbert's Oratory and was restored in the 19th century. Lit by a beautiful stained-glass window the serene interior is decorated with oak panelling, screens and stalls brought from Durham Cathedral. The font in the foreground is a favourite nesting place for Arctic terns.

Dunstanburgh
(above)

Dunstanburgh's strategic importance can easily be seen from the vantage point of her towers. Looking south towards the small village of Craster the coast sweeps southwards towards Newton and Howick eventually arriving at Alnmouth, Amble and Coquet Island. The most notable feature along its curtain wall is the Lilburn Tower, which is clearly visible for miles around. Dating from 1323 its ground floor would have held provisions while the upper floor provided accommodation for the garrison.

   In the early 1380s major alterations to the castle were carried out by John of Gaunt. Among these are the stark remains of the great gatehouse that, unusually, doubled as a keep; this still conveys the power of this wonderful building. It would have been necessary for any attacking force trying to gain access to the castle to go through this narrow passage and they would be exposed to fire from above and below. The castle was given to the Ministry of Works in 1929 and today it is in the care of English Heritage.

Alnmouth cross

This cross on the southern side of the
Aln estuary marks the site of the original
village church of Alnmouth. In 1806 a
great storm blew up which forced the
Aln to change course and cut the church
off from the village. In 1207 the village
was granted a charter for a port and a
market. In the 18th century the main
export was grain and many of the
granaries can still be seen, now converted
into houses. Imports into Alnwick
included slates, timber and guano. Once
derided by the preacher John Wesley as a
wicked place, today Alnmouth is a sleepy
little village at the mouth of the river Aln.

Beadnell *(left)*

The sun sets over the cobles nestling in
the harbour of Beadnell. This fishing port
is very unusual: despite the fact that it is
on the east coast, the harbour was built
so that it can only be entered by boats
approaching from the west.

The beach at Beadnell is capped at
its northern end by the harbour and limekilns. Dating from 1789 these huge kilns
were last used for lime production in the
1820s; later they were used for herring
curing. In the summer up to 60 local
fishermen worked the keel boats
operating out of the harbour often
accompanied by boats from Cornwall and
Scotland. Today, Beadnell is not only a
working fishing village but also one of the
region's most popular holiday beaches.

Alnwick Castle

Often called the Windsor of the North, the rolling fields and scattered copses betray the hand of the famous landscape gardener Capability Brown who laid out Alnwick's grounds in the 18th century. The 14th-century barbican at Alnwick is one of the most impressive in the country. Built by the Normans it was acquired by the de Vescys in 1090 and in 1309 passed into the hands of the Percys.

The castle was restored in the 19th century and today the walls look over the river Aln and the landscaped park below. Every Shrove Tuesday the two parishes of the town play each other here in a unique game of football, a tradition that goes back centuries. The lion of the Percy family stares at all who drive into the town from the north and thus gives the bridge its name. It figures prominently in Turner's painting of the castle by moonlight and offers superb views of the parkland. Although open to the public the castle remains the private family home of the Dukes of Northumberland.

The Tenantry Column

Standing some 83ft (25m) high the fine fluted stone Tenantry Column has an internal staircase leading to a gallery at the top. It was raised in 1816 by grateful tenants of the Duke of Northumberland, who reduced their rents after the Napoleonic wars to alleviate their hardship. The Duke then decided that if they could afford such a gesture they could afford the higher rents and he promptly raised them again. Ever since the column has been known locally as the "Farmer's Folly".

Alnwick Garden and Treehouse

Enclosed by walls which are 250 years old, Alnwick Garden is believed to be one of the largest walled gardens in the world. On entering the visitor is greeted by the Grand Cascade where 7,260 gallons of water per minute tumble down 27 weirs, disappearing into four large bell mouth openings, to reappear at the other side of a walkway in four "mounds" of water. The three large central jets reach a height of 20ft (6m), with 40 smaller jets sending water 15ft (5m) into the air. These are complemented by 80 side jets that create sweeping curves of water to the centre of the Cascade.

Outside the walls of the main garden is one of the world's largest wooden treehouses, an enormous structure of turret-topped buildings and amazing walkways in the sky that link the different sections.

The site on which Alnwick garden is built has had a colourful history, with gardens being planted here by leading contemporary designers.

Chillingham (below)

The large cannons that sit outside Chillingham Castle bear witness to the violent past of one of Northumberland's most fascinating castles. Now a stately home open to the public, Chillingham Castle has seen more than its fair share of border warfare and is reputed to be one of the most haunted houses in the county. Amongst the ghosts is Lady Mary Berkeley whose rustling dress can still be heard along the corridors and stairs accompanied by a chilling blast of air.

The present structure dates from 1344 when Sir Thomas Grey built a courtyard and curtain wall around an old pele tower. In 1590 the main entrance was moved to its present position, in preparation for the visit of King James VI of Scotland on his journey south to London for his coronation.

By the 1930s the castle had become neglected until Sir Humphrey Wakefield and Lady Mary Grey took over the estate and began the task of restoration. The castle is famous for its herd of wild Chillingham white cattle, the sole survivors of their species, who have been on the site for over 700 years.

Belsay Hall and Castle (above and below)

Sir Charles Monck was greatly influenced by the art and culture of the ancient Greeks. In 1817 he decided to build a Grecian-style house on his estate at Belsay and employed some of the finest craftsmen of the day to do so.

Belsay Hall has one of the most beautiful and fascinating gardens in Northumberland. It is full of corridors, arches and ravines with vines, ferns, palms and exotic and rare plants. In the late 19th and early 20th centuries Sir Charles' grandson Sir Arthur Middleton extended the garden and introduced rhododendrons and other plants new to the country at the time.

In the grounds of the estate is the original Belsay Castle, a conglomeration of building styles completed down through the ages. The original castle was a tower house built around 1360 which still has its battlements and arrow vents. In the early 17th century a two-storeyed range was built alongside and in 1717 a further wing was added although little remains of this extension today.

Blyth Beach

To the north and south of Blyth's harbour entrance are wide open beaches. Much of the coastline to the north consists of sand dunes with their typical grasses and habitats. Like other ports in Northumberland, Blyth owes its present size to the development of the coal industry, which reached its peak in the 1960s. Nowadays large wind vanes can be seen on the harbour wall supplying electricity. The row of nine 300kw Windmaster turbines generate green electricity. At the time, the turbines were the largest erected offshore in the world.

Amble harbour

Officially known as Warkworth harbour, Amble harbour was constructed in 1839 and owes its existence to its coal exports. Although one of Northumberland's most important fishing ports, Amble today is renowned for leisure sailing. Compared to other ports, however, Amble still has a large fishing fleet and is regarded as a traditional working port. The larger fishing boats that moor along the harbour wall land a variety of fish, crabs, lobsters and prawns and working cobles can still be seen in the inner harbour.

Hadrian's Wall

The defensive wall built between AD122-128 by the emperor Hadrian to defend the northernmost outpost of the Roman Empire stretches 73 miles (117km) from the Solway Firth to the river Tyne. The wall is 15ft (4m) high and would have been topped off by a further 6ft (2m) of timber. The wall had 16 forts, 18 mile-castles and many signal turrets. It was designated a World Heritage Site in 1987.

Housesteads *(right)*

Built when the Roman Empire was at its height, Housesteads is the best-preserved example of a Roman fort in the country. It held a garrison of around a thousand men, most of whom were German auxiliaries. Unlike other forts along the wall, Housesteads is built on quite a noticeable slope; the Romans sited their granaries on the highest part of the fort to keep the food inside dry. During the time of the reivers (cross-border raiders who were both Scots and English) Housesteads became a useful hiding place for raiders, cattle rustlers and their booty.

Sycamore Gap

The lone sycamore tree standing in a prominent position on Hadrian's Wall close to Steel Rigg gives the name to this well-known beauty spot, north of the A69 between Haltwhistle and Haydon Bridge. Sycamore Gap became famous when it was used as a location for scenes in the 1991 movie *Robin Hood: Prince of Thieves*, which starred Kevin Costner. The tree is 70 years old; in the film a great deal of work was needed to turn it into an English oak similar to those found in Sherwood Forest.

The wall near Whin Sill

The magnificent beauty of the winter landscape around Hadrian's Wall is seen above in this view looking towards Housesteads. The photograph reveals how the Romans made use of the steep slopes of the Whin Sill escarpment when the wall was under construction.

Birdoswald

This is one of the most spectacular locations of any fort on the Roman wall as it stands on a high spur of land overlooking the Irthing Gorge. You can still see parts of the original turf wall built in AD122. A small museum illustrates the lives of the soldiers who were stationed at this unfriendly outpost of empire.

Corbridge *(above)*

The bridge at Corbridge was built in 1674 and still gives access to one of Northumberland's most interesting towns. It was so well built that it was the only bridge on the Tyne to withstand the great flood of 1771 when it was said the water was so high that people could lean over the parapet and wash their hands. Corbridge is known for its quaint town centre and individual shops and is an ideal base to explore the beauty of Northumberland.

Prudhoe and Langley castles

The name Prudhoe means "proud hill". The castle which lies on the south bank of the Tyne is protected on the east by a steep ravine and is partly enclosed by a deep moat. It is first mentioned in 1173 when it was besieged by the Scots shortly after it was built by Odinel d'Umfreville.

William the Lion of Scotland besieged the castle again one year later. The castle remained a fortress of the Umfrevilles until 1381 when it passed to the Percys. By the 19th century the castle had fallen into disuse and is now in the care of English Heritage.

Langley Castle (right) looks much as it did when it was first built in 1364. It was the stronghold of the Lucy family but after only 50 years it was gutted by fire, perhaps on the orders of Henry IV. Since that time however the castle has been a fortress, a private house, a barracks during the Second World War and a girls' public school until it finally became the hotel it is today.

Countryside near Corbridge

Corbridge is particularly noted for its beauty and the town's parks and riverside walks are very popular. The Northumberland Show is held annually in the fields outside the town and draws visitors and exhibitors from all over the county.

One of the most important supply depots for Hadrian's Wall was at Corbridge just north of the present town. It occupied a strategic position at the point where the Stanegate, the road running parallel with the wall towards Carlisle, met Dere Street, the main road into Scotland where it crossed the Tyne. Much of the stone from the site was used to build Hexham Abbey and parts of Corbridge itself.

Kielder Water *(below)*

The largest artificial lake in Europe, Kielder Water holds a staggering 200 billion litres of water which supplies the people and the industries of the north-east. Kielder Castle was built in 1775 as a shooting lodge for the Duke of Northumberland and now acts as the main visitor centre for the park, which has become a centre for recreational activities such as sailing, canoeing, cycling and birdwatching. The main species in the forest is Sitka spruce; this hardy tree survives well in this hostile upland environment and accounts for 75% of the forest area.

Coquetdale *(above)*

Coquetdale has a timeless air about it; with its bracken and rocky outcrops it is easy to imagine the valley's earliest human inhabitants carving the many cup and ring mark patterns, and horsemen driving stolen cattle along the river's edge.

Harbottle dominates the valley and is home to the castle where Margaret, Countess of Lennox, grandmother of James VI of Scotland and I of England, was born. The valley offers stunning scenery all year round and is part of the Northumberland National Park.

A few miles up the valley, where the Coquet meets the Alwin, is Alwinton, now famous for its Border Shepherds show, the last of the many agricultural shows that are held each year. Heading north out of the village is Clennel Street, one of the great droving roads that heads northwards to the border.

Yeavering Bell hill fort *(right)*

The largest Iron Age hill fort in the region, Yeavering Bell lies on the edge of the Cheviot Hills some three miles north of Wooler, enclosing some 13 acres (5.2ha). Its most remarkable feature is a massive stone-walled rampart, in places some 12ft (4m) wide, which encloses much of the summit and can be easily seen from the roads below.

Inside the fort are traces of 130 hut platforms. Beyond the main wall which encloses all of the summit are additional defensive stone outworks on the east and west sides. An entire town existed here some 2,000 years ago until it was abandoned sometime around the 1st century. It is not clear why but the walls do appear to have been deliberately flattened which suggests that the Romans may have destroyed the fort.

After the Roman withdrawal, the fort was reoccupied for a time remaining in use and being rebuilt at least four or five times, up until the reign of King Edwin in the 7th century.

Seaton Sluice Sands *(left)*

To the north of the harbour of Seaton Sluice is an area of dunes and a long sandy beach. The sand dunes cover an area called Hartley Links which forms a protective barrier between the sea and the land. There have been attempts to protect this fragile environment by planting marram grass to help bind the dunes and stabilise them. This is a wonderful area in which to walk and enjoy views of the harbour and beach.

Cullercoats *(right)*

The lifeboat station at Cullercoats must be one of the most colourfully decorated in the country. The lifeboat was established here in 1852 and the boat today is an inshore inflatable lifeboat that can reach 32 knots.

Cullercoats was originally a small fishing village and at one point had 15 cobles operating from the port; salt was also exported from here and it is recorded that the *Fortune of Whitby* sailed in July 1726 with 21 tons on board. Cullercoats was particularly popular with artists in the later years of the 19th century and work by the "Cullercoats Group" is now sought after by collectors. The Dove Marine Laboratory, an important facility for marine science, is sited here.

St Mary's Lighthouse *(below)*

Lit up at night, St Mary's Lighthouse not only makes a beautiful reflection in the rock pools at low tide but also reveals the causeway which crosses the dangerous rocks surrounding the island. Built in 1898 and some 120ft (36.5m) high, the lighthouse has a birdwatching hide and visitor centre open to the public. As well as a popular recreational destination it houses permanent and changing exhibitions and offers educational facilities for local people. It is thought that the monks from Tynemouth had a chapel on the north side of the island and also a tower with an additional storey where a lantern was kept burning.

From the light's platform the view of the coast slips away southwards towards Whitley Bay, Cullercoats and the mouth of the Tyne. Opposite the island, sometimes called Bate's or Bait Island, is Curry's Point, where the body of Michael Curry was hung in chains after he was executed for murder in 1739.

Elsdon

The Vicar's pele tower at Elsdon was built about 1400 and has walls 9ft (3m) thick. The village also has the spectacular remains of a Norman motte and bailey castle and is noted for its large sloping green and the nearby Winter's Gibbet. One of the rectors here was the Reverend Charles Dodgson who, from 1762 to 1765, was a tutor to the Duke of Northumberland's son. He was also the great grandfather of Lewis Carroll, the author of Alice in Wonderland.

Tynemouth Castle

The massive gatehouse at Tynemouth Castle is an extension of the fortifications of the priory. The first castle here was a motte and bailey affair with a wooden palisade. The middle ages saw the castle act as a place of sanctuary. Charles I strengthened its defences and during the Civil War it was besieged and captured by both Royalist and Parliamentary forces. During the Second World War the castle was used as the base for a coastal defence unit.

Tynemouth Priory

Perched on a clifftop, Tynemouth Priory is protected both by the sea and Tynemouth Castle, and is one of the largest fortified sites in the country. Originally the site was occupied by a 7th-century Saxon church, renowned as the burial place of St Oswin, king and martyr. The early monastery was sacked by the Danes in 800. The present buildings date from 1085 when a group of Benedictine monks from at St Albans arrived here; the monastery was finally completed at the end of the 13th century. The monks amassed great wealth from the coal industry which they used to finance the building work.

North Shields

The fish quay at North Shields with its distinctive lighthouse (left) is one of the best-known views in the north-east. Although much diminished from earlier days, fishing is still important here. Today the town remains an important commercial centre and the modern Royal Quays shopping centre attracts thousands.

North Shields has had its share of tragedy in wartime: in 1941 a single bomb from a lone German raider scored a direct hit on the air-raid shelter of the Wilkinson Lemonade factory killing 105 people.

Further down the coast is the Souter Lighthouse. Opened in 1871, it was the first in the world to use electric current. To the north is the Leas: two and a half miles of cliffs, beaches and grassland with spectacular views. To the south Whitburn Coastal Park offers similar pleasures. The lighthouse was decommissioned in 1988 and now belongs to the National Trust. One of the cottages has been restored to provide a fascinating insight into the past lives of the lighthouse-keepers.

South Shields

Marsden Rock is sited on a beautiful stretch of the north-east coast and is one of the most spectacular rock formations in Britain. Renowned for the thousands of pairs of seabirds that nest here, the rock was even more dramatic prior to 1996 when the arch that joined the present two stacks collapsed into the sea.

The rocks here are reputedly haunted by the ghost of John the Jibber. It is rumoured that he died a lingering death suspended in a bucket halfway down the cliff, having betrayed his fellow smugglers to the customs men.

As well as the beaches, the Marsden Grotto is popular. The origins of this pub date back to 1782, when an Allenheads leadminer nicknamed "Jack the Blaster" came to work in the limestone quarries at Marsden.

Segedunum *(below)*

The 100ft high (30.5m) viewing tower at Segedunum, Wallsend offers amazing views of the most easterly Roman fort of Hadrian's Wall, sections of the wall and the river Tyne. The site also has a working reconstructed Roman bath-house, the only one of its kind in Britain. Segedunum is the largest Roman museum on Hadrian's Wall and features site finds together with the latest computer interactive displays. The wall originally finished at Newcastle before the Romans decided to extend it a further 3.5 miles (5.5km) eastwards to the new fort at Wallsend, housing a unit of infantry soldiers and cavalry-troopers.

Arbeia Roman Fort and Museum

Four miles to the east of the end of Hadrian's Wall at South Shields, Arbeia guarded the entrance to the river Tyne from incursion by sea. Constructed around AD160 it played a vital role in the running of the wall. Originally built to house a cavalry garrison, its role changed around AD208 when it became the military supply depot for the 17 forts along the wall and other parts of the Roman frontier defensive system such as watchtowers and signalling stations.

Millennium Bridge at night

The lighting beneath the pedestrian deck of the Gateshead Millennium Bridge, which performed its first tilt in November 2000, causes an almost mirror-like appearance on the surface of the slow moving river Tyne. The arch is lit with a series of high-powered lights which change colour, the display blending in seamlessly with the buildings of Newcastle and Gateshead on either bank. The bridge creates a circular promenade in conjunction with the Swing Bridge that allows people to enjoy and appreciate both of the newly revitalised banks of the river. This walk is especially popular at night when separate sections are illuminated in different colours.

Building the bridge

Europe's largest floating crane, the Asian Hercules II, transported the bridge six miles up the river to its present position in November 2000. In certain places the bridge was wider than the river and it had to be turned sideways to continue its journey.

When it was opened in 2001 the Millennium Bridge had cost over £22m. Amazingly the bridge can be raised and lowered, silently, in only four minutes. When open, it allows ships 82ft (25m) headroom, the same as the clearance of the Tyne Bridge. When closed the clearance is 15.5ft (4.7m) and the navigation channel is 98.5ft (30m) wide, equal to that of the neighbouring Armstrong Swing Bridge.

Tyne bridges

An autumn sunset (above) bathes the Tyne and her bridges in an orange light. The Tyne bridges hold a special place in the history of the north-east; they have performed a vitally important role in the region's social and economic development throughout the ages. Each of the bridges has its own story to tell. The Swing Bridge opened in 1876 and was specially designed to allow large ships to pass upriver. The High Level Bridge, which opened in 1850, is one of the most important structures in the history of the British railway system. Robert Stephenson's bridge brought Newcastle into the London-Edinburgh railway link and confirmed the East Coast line as the major rail route between the two cities. Opened by King George V in 1928 the Tyne Bridge is used by approximately 60,000 vehicles a day and was originally intended to have massive triumphal arches at each end. It is now associated with the swarming mass of runners crossing it as part of the Great North Run.

Civic Centre

Bathed in a blue light that seems to represent the waters of the Tyne, Newcastle's Civic Centre reflects much of the history and culture of this great city. Twelve seahorse heads cast in bronze, part of Newcastle's coat of arms, adorn the top of the tower. The heads are approximately 5ft (1.5m) in diameter. Sixteen feet (5m) up the exterior wall is a sandstone statue of the river god (below), with water pouring out of his outstretched hand.

This imposing building has three wings arranged round a courtyard and a 12-storey main block to the north, capped by a copper lantern and beacon and a circular debating chamber to the west. King Olaf of Norway officially opened the Civic Centre in 1968. The city's links with the countries of Scandinavia are symbolised by the bronze statue of swans soaring into flight in the courtyard.

Art in Newcastle

The splendid Baltic Arts Centre (left) is a superb addition to the Newcastle-Gateshead scene. This magnificent warehouse was formerly a flour mill, where grain was stored before being loaded onto ships for export. The £46m arts centre opened in 2002 and has 3,000sq m of galleries, a cinema, lecture theatre, workshops and artists' studios. It is the largest venue for contemporary art outside London. The Millennium Bridge has provided a stylish link between the Newcastle and Gateshead Quays for pedestrians and visitors.

Art has become far more accessible to the public either side of the river, from outdoor attractions such as the Swirle Pavilion and the bronze Vulcan statue (right) by Sir Eduardo Paolozzi, to exhibitions by artists at the Baltic.

The Sage

The Sage Gateshead is a centre for music and the performing arts. The dramatic glass and stainless steel building on the south Quayside was designed by Sir Norman Foster and has been likened to a "resting armadillo". It has a 1,700-seat hall plus a flexible 450-seat auditorium and the interior of the building with its innovative walkways, stairs and brilliant lighting is a superb example of modern architecture.

Around the front and sides of the Sage is a glazed concourse that provides stunning views of the Quayside and river. The roof of this incredible building holds over 3,500sq m of glass; this allows light to flood the building during the day and provides a colourful spectacle when the building is viewed from outside after dark.

City panorama

This view taken from the castle keep towards Newcastle's Moot Hall shows many of the major sights of both Newcastle and Gateshead through the ages, from the old city walls in the foreground to the Tyne Bridges and the new buildings of the Quayside in the distance. The city's 13th-century walls butt up against the Moot Hall now standing in the old courtyard of the castle, opposite the keep.

William Stokoe designed the hall in 1810 in a Greek Doric and Pediment style. Further back, the 19th-century Swing Bridge is dominated by the 20th-century Tyne Bridge in the centre of the photograph. From the 21st century the "glass armadillo" of the Sage Gateshead on the far bank of the river and the curve of the Gateshead Millennium Bridge catch the eye.

St James' Park (above) and the Castle keep

The stadium of Newcastle FC dominates the northern part of Newcastle. First built in 1880, it has been completely redeveloped in recent years and now has a capacity of more than 52,000.

The keep (right) is all that remains today of the "new castle" that gave the city its name. It was constructed as part of the rebuilding in stone of the castle carried out by Henry II and took 10 years to complete. Even today, this imposing structure gives an impression of immense military power. Newcastle Corporation supplied cannons to the keep to be fired on ceremonial occasions. This ended in tragedy in 1812 when one of the cannons exploded and a gunner was blown over the parapet. Next to the keep is the Black Gate, which dates back to before 1649. The slots which held the counterweights of the drawbridge are still clearly visible.

Grey Street

Built in 1836 by John Dobson and Richard Grainger, Grey Street has often been referred to as "England's finest street". Indeed the imposing Regency buildings that sit either side of this gently curving thoroughfare have now become recognised as a style of architecture known as "Tyneside Classical". The heritage-led Grainger Town partnership has recently restored much of Newcastle city centre to its former glory including Grey Street. The pavements have been upgraded too, using Caithness stone from Scotland, Newcastle's original paving material.

In recent years Newcastle has become one of the loveliest illuminated cities in the country. City centre streets have been enhanced at night by lighting, especially now that the beautiful stonework has been cleaned and its natural colours exposed. One example of this is the Theatre Royal; its distinctive portico has six massive Corinthian columns rising up from enormous moulded plinths supporting a classical triangular pediment bearing the Royal Coat of Arms. The original Theatre Royal was located on Mosley Street; keen to incorporate a theatre into his newly designed city centre, Richard Grainger paid hefty compensation to close the old theatre and relocate it to Grey Street. The new theatre opened in February 1837.

Gibside *(above and right)*

The Gibside Estate was the property of the coal magnate George Bowes who developed this great "forest garden" over 200 years ago. It is now owned by the National Trust and offers the visitor 15 miles of woodland and walks beside the river Derwent with dramatic romantic ruins. Gibside Chapel was designed by James Paine and built as a mausoleum in the 1760s for George Bowes. Famous for its unusual three-tiered pulpit, it has today become a popular venue for weddings.

The chapel was consecrated in 1812 and the mausoleum beneath the chapel is a plain circular vaulted chamber with a central column from which burial niches radiate around the walls. An avenue extends from the chapel to an obelisk with a statue of British Liberty also designed by Paine in 1757.

Jesmond Dene *(below)*

A wooded valley which runs alongside the river Ouseburn between South Gosforth and Jesmond Vale, Jesmond Dene is rich in wildlife. Its exotic trees and shrubs, miles of footpaths and waterfalls provide a wonderful "green corridor" close to the heart of the city. In 1835 William Armstrong, the famous north-east industrialist, acquired the land partly to build a banqueting house and also to build Jesmond Dean as a family home. By the 1870s Armstrong was spending much of his time at his new home at Cragside; in 1883 he donated the site to the city of Newcastle. Unfortunately the banqueting house is now a ruin and Jesmond Dean is no longer in existence.

The Hoppings *(right)*

The huge fairground called the Hoppings is best seen at night when tens of thousands of coloured lightbulbs burn brightly across the Town Moor. The Newcastle Hoppings is Europe's largest travelling fair. Local folklore has it that the rain that often accompanies the fair is the result of a Romany curse.

The Temperance Fair held on the Town Moor was the forerunner of the Hoppings. There were children's games, sports and music and at the end of the day those gathered would feast and drink and then dance or "hop" around bonfires to the music of local pipers or fiddlers. These gatherings or fairs consequently became known as the "Hoppings".

Saltwell Towers

Saltwell Park, based in the heart of Gateshead, is one of Britain's finest examples of a Victorian park. Opened to the public in 1876 when the park was bought for the people of the town by Gateshead Corporation, it is still known as "the people's park". Saltwell Park contains 11 listed buildings and monuments, including the magnificent Gothic mansion of Saltwell Towers and its gardens which were built between 1850 and 1862, one of two contrasting Victorian landscapes here. The other is the mid 19th-century parkland designed by Edward Kemp which consists of a series of gardens in different styles, from an open meadow to a formal Italianate garden.

Angel of the North

Constructed from sections transported to the site in 1998 and overlooking the A1, it is estimated that at least 90,000 motorists a day pass Antony Gormley's *Angel of the North*; it can also be seen clearly by rail passengers on the East Coast mainline from London to Edinburgh. Few realise the statue is actually hollow to allow for internal inspections with an access door on one of the shoulder blades, and that it is built on the site of a former colliery pit-head baths. It is taller than four double-decker buses and its wings are almost as long as those of a Jumbo jet. The Angel is made of weather resistant Cor-ten steel, containing a small amount of copper, which forms a patina on the surface that mellows with age; it contains enough steel to make four Chieftain tanks. In its exposed, hillside position, the statue has been designed to withstand winds of 100mph.

Sunderland Bridge

Built in 1929 the Wearmouth Bridge crosses the river Wear linking Sunderland with Hylton and Monkwearmouth on the north of the river. When it was erected in 1796, the original bridge was the longest single-span cast iron bridge in the world. The railway bridge behind was built in 1879 and extended the railway south from Monkwearmouth to the centre of Sunderland.

In the mid 17th century the proximity of the Durham coalfield to the city necessitated new port facilities and an expansion in shipbuilding. By 1840 there were 65 shipyards on the river and Sunderland took its place as the biggest shipbuilding port in the world. The last coalmine, the Monkwearmouth Colliery, closed in 1993 and today is the site of the Stadium of Light, home to Sunderland FC. Sunderland was awarded city status in 1992.

Like many industrial cities of the north-east, Sunderland has undergone a renaissance in its town planning. In addition to riverside walks it now boasts a new marina complex.

Hylton Castle

Hylton Castle is a medieval gatehouse and tower in Hylton Dene, Sunderland. The castle stood guard over an important ferry crossing of the Wear and is most famous for its ghost called the "Cauld Lad o' Hylton", a stable boy cruelly murdered by his master. The keep, four main walls and part of the chapel are all still standing. Over the years, the Castle and Dene had become neglected and vandalised. In 1992 a group of local residents set to work restoring the Dene and planning for its future. It is now in the care of English Heritage.

Sunderland Winter Gardens

Sunderland's Winter Gardens house a superb botanical collection of over 1,500 plants of 146 species in naturalistic settings under a single-span 98.5ft (30m) dome. The gardens display samples of many important plants from around the world and visitors can take a staircase or scenic lift up to a treetop walkway where they can look down into an amazing rainforest canopy below. The gardens also house a number of exotic palms from countries such as Australia, Madagascar and Malaysia. The Winter Gardens are linked to Sunderland's remodelled museum and the upgraded and re-landscaped Mowbray Park in the city centre.

Penshaw Monument *(below)*

Built in 1844 by private subscription and designed by John and Benjamin Green of Newcastle, the Penshaw Monument is unusual in that it has no inscription. Built in the form of a 100ft (30.5m) long, 50ft (15m) wide and 70ft (21m) high ruined Greek temple, the monument is based on the Thesion, the Temple of Theseus in Athens. It commemorates John George Lambton, first Earl of Durham (known as Radical Jack). Located opposite Herrington Country Park, its high position astride Penshaw Hill gives views as far afield as Durham Cathedral and the north Pennines.

Sunderland Empire

The Sunderland Empire with its distinctive tower topped off with a turreted dome and silver globe is a well-loved landmark in the city. The Empire's internal layout is virtually unique in theatre design since the side "slipper seats" almost border the stage. The foundation stone of the theatre was laid on September 29 1906 and in July 1907 the Edwardian music hall favourite Vesta Tilley declared the Empire open when performing on stage.

The theatre was originally called the Empire Palace and on opening it had a 3,000-seat auditorium. Today the capacity has been reduced to around 1,900. Legendary comedy stars Stan Laurel and Charlie Chaplin performed here; tragically, on the opening night of *The Mating Season* in 1976, the actor Sid James of *Carry On* fame died on stage after suffering a heart attack. In 2004 the Empire re-opened after a £4.5m refit with a production of Andrew Lloyd Webber's *Starlight Express*. The work carried out during a nine-month closure included the complete rebuilding of the stage, the construction of a new orchestra pit plus work to the roof and backstage areas.

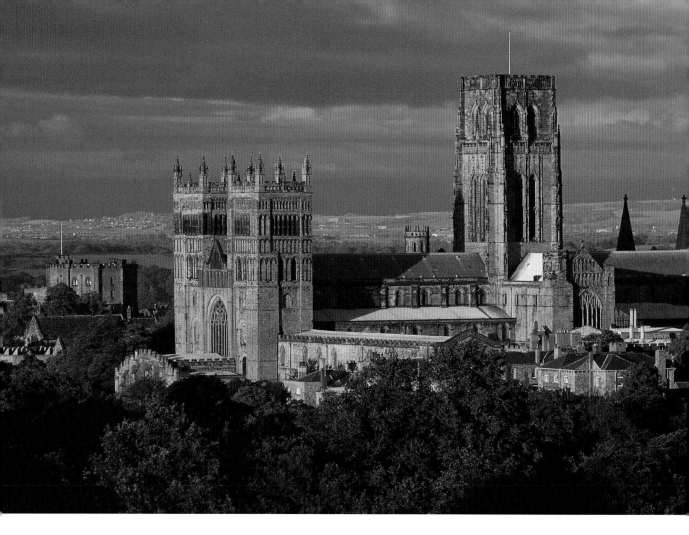

Durham Cathedral

Begun by Bishop William of Calais in 1093, Durham Cathedral is an outstanding example of Romanesque architecture. The cathedral is famous for the spiral and zig-zag decorated columns in the nave, whilst the arches that divide the nave into the separate sections are amongst the earliest pointed examples in Europe. The cathedral has been a centre for pilgrimage throughout its 900-year history. It contains the tombs of St Cuthbert, the saintly seventh-century bishop of Lindisfarne and that of the Venerable Bede, the first English historian, which were placed there in 1370. There have been occasions over the centuries when the cathedral has suffered damage and vandalism. The 14th-century altar screen originally contained 107 alabaster figures but many were vandalised in the 16th century. In 1650 further damage was caused when Cromwell imprisoned 4,000 Scots there. One of the most beautiful features of the cathedral today is the rose window with its central core depicting Christ surrounded by the apostles; it was created in the 15th century and reconstructed in the 18th.

Durham Castle *(right)*

Durham Castle is a fine example of the Norman motte and bailey style of fortification. Building began in 1072 with a circular keep on top of the hill overlooking the town as a part of William the Conqueror's plan to pacify the region; the castle was enlarged in 1174. During the middle ages, Durham was one of a number of castles spread throughout the north to counter the threat of invasion from the Scots. Later it was taken over as the principal residence of the Bishops of Durham or the Prince Bishops as they were known, since they administered the county on behalf of the Crown. It was they who built the magnificent halls and chapel, rare survivors of secular Norman splendour. In the 1830s the bishops left the castle and it became part of the University of Durham.

Bowes Museum (*right*)

This famous museum in Barnard Castle originated in a private foundation created between 1862 and 1875 by John and Josephine Bowes. It was conceived and purpose-built as a public art gallery by the French architect Jules Pellechet and opened in 1892. The building is designed in the style of a French chateau and has public galleries on three floors and a collection of European fine and decorative arts from the middle ages to early Victorian times. There is particular emphasis on the arts of France including items from the Bowes' home in Paris. Perhaps the best-known exhibit in the museum is the famous Silver Swan, a life-size musical automaton comprising a clockwork mechanism covered in silver plumage above a music box.

Housed in a typically French grand chateau, Bowes puts the visitor in mind of grand houses in the French countryside. It has some of the best collections of European art in Britain. French, Spanish and Italian paintings are a feature of the collection together with European ceramics and textiles. The museum also houses collections of archaeological finds from County Durham and artefacts showing the social history of Teesside. Another of Bowes' attractions is a fine collection of posters by Toulouse Lautrec.

Bishop Auckland

Bishop Auckland is situated at the confluence of the rivers Wear and Gaunless and has been the site of an important market since medieval times. As the name implies, the town has been the seat of the Bishops of Durham since the 12th century. Bishop Auckland grew up around the gates of Auckland Castle which is still the official residence of the Bishops of Durham. Originally a Norman manor house and hunting lodge, today the castle stands in its own park east of the town's marketplace. The French-style town hall situated in the marketplace is a Grade I listed building. The main street in Bishop Auckland follows the course of the Roman Dere Street which led to the Roman fort of Binchester, just to the north of the town.

High Force

Not only is the waterfall of High Force an incredible visual spectacle it is also memorable for its sound, where the mumbling of the rapids turns into the dramatic ceaseless roaring boom of the water hitting the plunge pool beneath. Here the river Tees plunges 70ft (21m), making it the highest unbroken waterfall in the country. The water is brown, peaty and very cold, and forms impressive whirlpools. Beneath the falls is one of the largest remaining juniper woods in the country.

In addition to High Force there are two other waterfalls on this stretch of the Tees. Low Force is found about three miles away, whilst to the west approximately four miles away is Cauldron Snout, the highest "broken" waterfall in England. The cascade drops 200ft (61m) down a 450ft (137m) long series of rock steps. The name "force" comes from a Norse word meaning a waterfall.

Lumley Castle

Lumley Castle is a magnificent building set within nine acres of parkland, overlooking the river Wear and situated near Chester-le-Street. It was built in 1392 as a manor house and was later converted by Sir Ralph Lumley to the castle that can be seen today. Sir Ralph built four great corner towers and the intervening buildings as well as the main gateway on the east. Local legend has it that Lumley is haunted by Lily Lumley, a 14th-century lady of the manor and wife of Sir Ralph, who was apparently thrown down a well by two priests after she refused to convert to Catholicism when her husband was absent as Governor of Berwick.

In the 18th century the basement of the south-west tower was altered by Sir John Vanbrugh, the architect of Blenheim Palace and Seaton Delaval Hall in Northumberland. Today the castle is a hotel. It is often used by visiting international cricket teams, some of whom have checked out early because of the supposed ghostly goings on!

Stockton-on-Tees

The lights of Stockton's Teesquay Millennium Footbridge reflect on the waters of the river as the sun sets slowly behind. Stockton can trace its origins back to Saxon times whilst its market is first recorded as being held in 1310. The town is well known for its railway connections; it also made another tremendous impact on the history of the world when in 1826 John Walker invented the friction match. The great comic and music hall entertainer Will Hay was born in Stockton and the famous Conservative politician and prime minister, Harold Macmillan, the Earl of Stockton, represented the town as its MP for many years.

The Tees Barrage has created a stretch of, high-quality deep water making the river Tees suitable for watersports including sailing, rowing, wind-surfing, water-skiing, kayaking and canoeing. A man-made white-water course can also be found on the Tees.

Darlington

Darlington is well-known for its parks and leafy suburbs and despite its long history, dating from Saxon times, the town centre mostly consists of Victorian and 20th-century buildings. A sublime exception is the 12th-century Church of St Cuthbert, which stands on the banks of the river Skerne. The world's first public railway opened here on September 27 1825; as well as carrying coal to Stockton, the train had room for 600 passengers. Today Darlington's railway history is celebrated by a brick sculpture (above). Created in 1997 by David Mach, the sculpture contains 185,000 bricks and weighs 15,000 tonnes. It is modelled on the *Mallard*, the 1938 steam locomotive that reached a speed of 126mph, and was the long-time holder of the world rail speed record.

Middlesbrough *(left)*

The setting sun casts an eerie glow over the river Tees and Middlesbrough's famous Transporter Bridge. The bridge dominates the city's skyline and, with a clearance of 160ft (48m), was originally designed to allow tall ships to pass beneath. Opened on October 17 1911 by Prince Arthur of Connaught, this unique bridge with its central cradle that ferries cars and pedestrians across the river has become Middlesbrough's icon. Its gondola can carry 200 people or six cars and one minibus across the river in just two and a half minutes.

Staithes

The isolated and picturesque fishing village of Staithes developed on the end of a narrow headland, so most of the old town is clustered around the base of the cliffs, close to the water's edge. The alleys and little cottages of the village have remained much as they were in their 19th-century heyday, when over 200 boats fished out of Staithes. As a young man, in 1745, Captain Cook was apprenticed in Staithes; visitors can discover more about his history by visiting the Captain Cook and Staithes Heritage Centre, a converted chapel in the town.

In the late 19th century, when the railway opened up the east coast, Staithes became a magnet for Victorian tourists.

In a similar way to Cullercoats in Northumberland, the village attracted a large number of number of artists who became known as the Staithes Group. Well-known members of the group include Dame Laura Knight and Joseph Bagshawe and their work can be found in major collections including Tate Britain in London.

Saltburn

The beach at Saltburn is a popular venue for surfing and is famous for its attractive walks. Tides can be treacherous here and care needs to be taken when walking beneath the 365ft (111m) high Huntcliff. Saltburn was once a fashionable resort for the Victorians with its own rail link and formal gardens.

A miniature railway which still exists was constructed at around the same time. Just behind the seafront an Italianate garden and an ancient wooded area called Rifts Wood make up the Saltburn Valley gardens; they merge with a nature reserve and offer the visitor a superb display of both ornamental plants and wildflowers. The town and beach were once a hotbed of smuggling and many reminders of this activity can still be seen in Saltburn.

Saltburn Pier is the only remaining pier on the north-east coast and is now practically half its original length due to the pounding of the sea over the years. Completed in 1869 it was originally 1,400ft (427m) long; after restoration it was reopened in 1978 at its present length of 681ft (208m). It was however still in need of repair and further restoration work was completed in 2001.

First published in 2009 by Myriad Books Limited
35 Bishopsthorpe Road, London SE26 4PA

Photographs copyright © Graeme Peacock except those by Mike Kipling listed below

Graeme Peacock has asserted his right under the Copyright, Designs and Patents Act 1998 to be identified as the author of this work.

Photographs on pages 31 and 32 by Mike Kipling Photography.

www.mikekipling.com

ISBN 1 84746 247 2

Designed by Jerry Goldie Graphic Design

Printed in China
www.myriadbooks.com

Inventions That Shaped the World

THE CAMERA

TRUDI STRAIN TRUEIT

Franklin Watts
A Division of Scholastic Inc.
New York • Toronto • London • Auckland • Sydney
Mexico City • New Delhi • Hong Kong
Danbury, Connecticut

For William, whose photographs touch my soul

Photographs © 2006: Art Resource, NY: 24 (Bridgeman-Giraudon), 16 (HIP), 49 (Réunion des Musées Nationaux), 42, 47 (Victoria & Albert Museum, London); Bridgeman Art Library International Ltd., London/New York: 13 (Deir el-Medina, Thebes, Egypt), 40 (National Museum of Photography, Film & Television); Classic PIO Partners: cover left, chapter opener-antique camera; Corbis Images: 26, 61 (Bettmann), 7 (Kevin P. Casey), 64 (Jon Feingersh); Getty Images/Hulton Archive: 41 (Spencer Arnold), 45 (Eadweard Muybridge), 19; Library of Congress: cover bottom right, 30, 43 52; Mary Evans Picture Library: 51; Peter Arnold Inc./ Alfred Pasieka: 37; Photo Researchers, NY/Mehau Kulyk: 65; Superstock, Inc.: cover top right, chapter opener-contemporary camera (Nicholas Eveleigh), 10 (Explorer); The Art Archive/ Picture Desk: 20 (Marc Charmet), 55 (National Archives, Washington D.C.), 54 (Laurie Platt Winfrey); The Image Works: 66 (Amanda Morris), 35, 59, 63 (NMPFT/SSPL), 23 (SSPL), 62 (Topham).

Illustration by J. T. Morrow

Cover design by The Design Lab
Book production by The Design Lab

Library of Congress Cataloging-in-Publication Data
Trueit, Trudi Strain.
  The camera / Trudi Strain Trueit.
    p. cm. — (Inventions that shaped the world)
  Includes bibliographical references and index.
  ISBN 0-531-12409-6 (lib.bdg.)   0-531-13900-X (pbk.)
  1. Cameras—History—Juvenile literature. I. Title. II. Series.
  TR250.T77 2006
  771.3—dc22   2005026271